Teacher's Book

Gillian Howell

Rising Stars UK Ltd.
7 Hatchers Mews, Bermondsey Street, London SE1 3GS
www.risingstars-uk.com

nasen House, 4/5 Amber Business Village, Amber Close,
Amington, Tamworth, Staffordshire B77 4RP

Published 2011

Reprinted 2013 (twice), 2014

Editor: Deborah Kespert
Text design and typesetting: Clive Sutherland
Cover design: Burville-Riley Partnership
Editorial consultant: Lorraine Petersen

British Library Cataloguing in Publication Data.
A CIP record for this book is available from the British Library

ISBN: 978-1-84680-982-8

Printed in the UK by Ashford Colour Press, Ltd.

Contents

Introduction to All Star High   4

Working with reluctant reading groups   6

Role-play with reluctant reader groups   8

The All Star High eBooks   8

Teaching Notes and PCMs for each reader

HELP!   9

BAD   12

TROUBLE   15

THRILLER   18

SUPERSTAR   21

RESCUE   24

FIGHT   27

SHOUT!   30

CRIMINAL   33

FAME   36

Reading record   39

Character cards   40

Introduction to All Star High

There are ten books in the *All Star High* series. The stories can be read in any order as each story has a stand-alone plot and a clear resolution.

However, it is suggested that *HELP!* is read first, in order to establish the background and setting of the series.

The books in the series are: *BAD, TROUBLE, THRILLER, SUPERSTAR, RESCUE, FIGHT, SHOUT!, CRIMINAL, HELP!* and *FAME*.

Strong characters

The main characters are Jacky Singh, Tom Caplan, Natalie Caplan, Zeke Porter, Aaron Farmer, Claire Stevens, Callum Murphy and Becca Grey. They are all friends who had previously met at an under-12s music club. They all attend All Star High, a performing arts school, and have formed a group called the Gang-Stars. The Gang-Stars support and help each other out when they have a problem. Each story focuses on two main characters while the other characters feature in a background role.

Jacky is a classical violinist. She is feisty, imaginative and determined to be a success.

Tom's main talent is as a drummer. He is also a songwriter and has a band called Chasing Trouble. He sometimes gets things wrong because he is reluctant, or unable, to read information in posters or emails.

Natalie is Tom's talented little sister. She is unconventional and doesn't follow the crowd. Her skills are in dancing and singing, and she desperately wants to be a superstar.

Zeke is a talented dancer, particularly as a street dancer. He has a grant to attend the school, comes from a poor background and used to be a member of a street gang.

Aaron is a singer and actor but feels he is in the shadow of his more talented cousin, Callum. He is very keen on martial arts.

Claire is into classical ballet and wants to become a famous ballerina. She takes her classes very seriously and gets annoyed by others who don't.

Callum is very self-confident. He is the best singer and actor in the school and knows it.

Becca also has a grant to attend the school. She has a good eye for design and studies lighting and set design.

Motivating storylines

Central to each plot of the *All Star High* stories is the theme of friendship. When the members of the Gang-Stars experience problems, one or more of the other members comes to their aid, sometimes in ways that mean they have to take a back seat in order to allow the other to succeed.

Each character is following a dream of becoming famous and successful, and running through the stories is a secondary theme that success can come in ways other than expected.

In several of the stories, the characters have to overcome adversity or fear by supporting a friend and find they have strengths of which they were unaware.

Fast-moving narratives

In order to keep the reading age relatively low, there is a limited amount of descriptive action in the stories. Instead the series pushes the action forwards using dialogue and repartee between the characters.

Specially designed text

The layout of the text on the page has been designed to encourage independent reading.

Thought-provoking themes

Each story has an underlying serious theme. It is suggested that the teacher examines these themes with their pupils as part of a whole-class or group discussion.

Satisfying reads

Each story in the *All Star High* series is approximately 2500 words long, providing a satisfying and worthwhile read for reluctant readers. The books are designed to encourage independent reading during a 20-minute lesson, with pauses for discussion.

Supportive teacher resources

Each story is supported by a range of activities. In addition to a story summary, this Teacher's Book includes a list of questions to ask when discussing the text to develop the pupils' comprehension skills. There are also drama and role-play suggestions, which help pupils to examine the story at a deeper level and to empathise with the characters.

There are two photocopy master (PCM) activities for each story. These encourage pupils to develop word and text level skills using the stories as starting points. The range of activities includes simple comprehension exercises, spelling games, free writing and extended writing activities, grammar exercises and cloze procedures. Extension activities allow for further independent writing.

Opportunities for writing

Reluctant readers are not necessarily reluctant writers. With this in mind, the photocopy masters have been designed to provide substantial opportunities for independent writing practice. They can be used independently or in paired activities where additional support is required. In the main, pupils may write on the photocopied sheet. However, the teacher may at his or her discretion feel it would be more appropriate for the pupil to copy out the work onto a separate sheet. Extension activities may be written on the back of the photocopied sheet, on separate paper or in notebooks as preferred.

In-built differentiation

The teaching resources offer opportunities to differentiate the work according to individual needs.

- The text interrogation questions cater for a range of abilities.
- Photocopy masters can be used in a variety of ways, e.g. independently, with 1:1 guidance, in pairs or in small groups. It may be appropriate for more able pupils to do the extension activities only.
- Role-play and drama activities allow for pupils to contribute as much or as little as they feel able to. At the end of each role-play, time should be spent discussing performances and making suggestions for improvements.

Assessment Focus chart relating to the PCMs

	AF1	AF2	AF3	AF4	AF5	AF6	AF7
HELP!	R		R				
BAD		W	W			W	
TROUBLE			W	W	R		
THRILLER		R			R		
SUPERSTAR		R				W	
RESCUE		W				W	
FIGHT		W			R		W
SHOUT!			R			W	
CRIMINAL		W	W			W	
FAME				R		W	

R = Reading AF   W = Writing AF

Working with reluctant reading groups

All Star High stories are ideal for reading with a single pupil or with small groups. When working with reluctant reading groups, it is important to give pupils a book at a suitable reading level. This is a book which presents the reader with a challenge of ten per cent, i.e. one word in ten presents a challenge to that pupil.

Strategies to use before reading
Book introduction

An effective book introduction is an important strategy as it can pave the way for the pupils into the book. Below are some suggestions for introducing a book. Some or all of these suggestions may be used.

- Read the title on the front cover with the pupils.
- Ask the pupils to find the author's name, the name of the illustrator, the name of the publisher and the ISBN.
- Ask the pupils to scan through the book to find the names of the main characters.
- Before starting a reading session, ask the pupils to find important or difficult words. They should practise reading them and work out what they mean.
- Ask the pupils to decide the genre of the book. Is it fiction or non-fiction? Is it crime or mystery, science fiction or romance? Once the pupils have decided on the genre, ask them to outline the likely conventions for that sort of writing.

Strategies to use during reading aloud

When reading aloud, pupils should be encouraged to try different strategies when they get stuck on a word. This is best done by encouraging them to question the text. Below are some suggested questions they could ask themselves.

Prompts for the pupil to use

- What word would make sense here?
- Does the sentence I have read sound right?
- Does the word look like another one that I know? If so, how would it sound?
- Did I get the right sound at the beginning of the word?
- Can I say the last part of the word correctly?
- Shall I break the word down into its sounds and then roll it back together?

It is important for the teacher, when listening to a pupil stuck on a word, to give just enough help to get the reading moving again. The teacher's comment should be short, and designed to remind the pupil of the self-help strategies they could use.

For instance, reminding a pupil to try sounding out a word, or checking for meaning, could be cued in with a simple phrase like 'Sound it out,' or 'Is it making sense?'

The teacher should remind the pupil that there is more than one way of solving the problem: a good phrase for this is 'Why don't you try a different way?'

Prompts for the teacher to use

- Does it look like a word you know already?
- Think about the meaning of the sentence.
- Look carefully at the first few letters of the word.
- Think of a word that makes sense and sounds right.
- Reread the sentence.
- Leave out the hard word and read on, then go back and try again.
- Break a long word up into smaller parts.
- Can you see a pattern of letters that you know in the word?
- Read everything on the left of my finger, now on the right. Can you roll the two bits of the word together?

Thinking strategies to help pupils develop their reading

It will help lower-aged readers improve their reading skills if they analyse the thoughts that pass through their heads as they read. These skills can be explicitly taught and teachers should seek to reinforce them at every opportunity.

Good readers can sense when they are beginning to lose track of what they are reading. As they become aware of the problem, they bring in strategies to compensate for it.

1 Reading ahead: skim-reading into the text to see if confusing information can be clarified.
2 Making inferences: guessing at the meaning of a word or phrase on the basis of textual clues and prior knowledge about genres of writing.
3 Rereading: rereading a difficult section to see if any important detail has been missed.
4 Suspending judgement: waiting to see if the text provides more clues before deciding on a meaning.

Lower-aged readers are more likely to panic than to use any of the thinking strategies above. Good readers watch themselves read and are aware when they slip into confusion. Poor readers have too much on their minds to notice the moment when they stop understanding the text. The following strategies will help them to stay calm and monitor their own thought process.

1 Show pupils how to ask themselves about the meaning of the text as they are reading it. Encourage them to ask themselves these questions:
    - Is there anything wrong with this story?
    - Is what I'm expecting to happen still happening? Is the story still making sense?

- What do I already know about this subject? What's new in this passage?

2   Ask the pupils to form a mental picture of the narrative. By working through the text section by section, they should be able to visualise what is happening. Share images within the group, talk about them or draw them.

3   Encourage pupils to construct summary sentences. After reading short sections of the text, ask them to write one sentence about the main thing that has just happened. This is a good way to keep pupils focused on the meaning of what is being read.

Dealing with the 'spotlight' phenomenon

If you work with any group of pupils, you might have noticed an interesting phenomenon. Individual pupils are able to give the right answer to a reading problem when it's not their turn to read aloud. They can prompt another pupil effortlessly, yet are frozen to the spot when it's their turn to read to the group. With the spotlight on them, they feel stressed. Below are some strategies to help reduce the 'spotlight' phenomenon.

Strategies to reduce the 'spotlight' effect

- Allow one pupil to help the reader by prompting them when they get stuck. It is useful to wait for ten seconds before letting this happen.
- Allow paired reading. Two pupils taking it in turns to read to each other helps reduce the spotlight effect. One pupil can be a great teacher of another, especially if they trust one another and have similar reading difficulties. Often, a pupil looking over a shoulder of a reader can read the difficult words for them and take away the tension of reading aloud.
- Try some 'quick free-reading'. One pupil reads a sentence or a paragraph before the teacher passes the reading on to somebody else. This may be done in a specific order or randomly among the group. It keeps pupils focused, as they wait for their turn, and relaxed because they know the spotlight will not be on them for long.
- Try choric reading. The group reads the text in unison. This gives weaker pupils a sense of fluency, without having to get every word correct.
- Try voluntary reading nomination. A pupil picks the next person to read after them. The pupil can read as much or as little as they want before selecting the next member of the group. This process creates an atmosphere of unpredictability and entertainment. The pupil is in control of how long the spotlight stays on them.

Using a variety of strategies

It is useful to engage a variety of strategies when teaching a group: questioning the pupils about the meaning of the text; prompting a pupil through a problem; encouraging fluent reading; checking that a pupil has mastered a problem area; asking for general opinions from volunteers in the group.

Using a variety of strategies helps to keep pupils involved in the lesson and creates a dynamic and positive atmosphere.

The importance of praise

When teaching reluctant readers, the importance of praise cannot be underestimated. If there is a high level of praise in a group, a positive momentum often develops and the readers start making fewer mistakes.

Praise coaxes the reluctant reader along, strengthens the important emotional and psychological bond between reader and adult, and creates a good psychological atmosphere for reading aloud to take place.

Praise that links with a merit system is also useful. Low-level, high-frequency rewards encourage engagement with a reading lesson. This is an additional incentive on top of verbal encouragement. Any system of reward linked to work at home is likely to lead to more reading practice taking place.

Praise that is linked to a specific achievement is especially effective in encouraging reluctant readers. It is important to let the pupils know what targets they are aiming for to improve their reading and to praise them when they have achieved them.

It is important to praise both a successful and an unsuccessful attempt. The pupils need to know that they are using the right strategy even when they get it wrong. Practising a strategy can be more important than getting the right answer.

Suggested reading improvement targets:

- thinking about what they are reading;
- noticing letter sounds;
- stopping if they make a mistake, rather than ploughing on;
- trying to work words out without asking the teacher every time they are stuck;
- rereading a phrase to try and get it right;
- looking for a pattern they know in an unfamiliar word;
- use the picture clues to help them;
- for pupils with a low concentration span, staying on task for a specific amount of time.

Role-play with reluctant reading groups

There is a drama/role-play activity for each of the *All Star High* stories. Drama through role-play is an excellent way of helping reluctant readers access a text. It has many benefits:

- It helps to bring out the meaning of complex language.
- It encourages 'reading between the lines' as it helps pupils question character, motivation and plot.
- It helps pupils to rehearse ideas before they try to read or write them down.
- It is entertaining and motivating.
- It encourages pupils to express themselves and communicate with others.

Some of the *All Star High* drama suggestions involve 'hot-seating', whereby a pupil is asked to come to the front of the group and assume the role of a character from the story. Then they are interviewed by the teacher and the rest of the class. Questioning somebody who is in role, or being questioned while in role, is an excellent way for pupils to explore the depth of their knowledge about the characters and the story.

The *All Star High* eBooks

Using electronic versions of books, eBooks, on handheld devices is a proven way of motivating and supporting less able and reluctant readers. Pupils, especially boys, love accessing books through the exciting technology that they use in other parts of their lives, making reading comparable with activities such as gaming and surfing the net.

A big advantage of using eBooks on handheld devices is the degree of privacy offered to the reader – peers cannot see which level of book pupils are reading, so there is no embarrassment about being on a book scheme aimed at younger or less able readers. This removes a major barrier to reading success. Pupils like using eBooks on handheld devices as people around them won't know if they are reading or playing an electronic game. And if a reader wants to keep rereading one title until they are comfortable to move on to another, no one need know they are still on the same book. Any potential stigma is avoided.

eBooks enable readers to choose the text size and typeface that suits them and to easily navigate books by jumping to the right chapter or page and using electronic bookmarks. Other simple-to-use tools include being able to add comments and questions to pages so that pupils can flag parts they didn't understand or particularly enjoyed. All this aids active reading and comprehension, as well as making reading enjoyable.

All ten books in the *All Star High* series can be accessed as eBooks. Not only can they be used on PDAs, but teachers can also display them for the whole class or a guided reading group on an interactive whiteboard, PC/Mac or laptop. You can explore books together, listen to automated audio, highlight sections, add comments and more.

HELP!

Story summary

Tom Caplan, a student at All Star High School, is in despair because the double bass player in his band has left just before a big competition. He persuades his friend Jacky Singh, a violinist, to step in. However, when they start to practise, Jacky finds her style of playing doesn't work with Tom's punk music. She suggests she 'mashes up' the music by adding some classical playing. The audience loves it, and Jacky joins Tom's band permanently.

Vocabulary and spelling

Tricky words: different, musician, worst, bass, piece, busy, competition, enough, February, choice, signed, weird, meant, guess, café, chords, fault, listen, audience, sure, friends

Hyphenated words: Gang-Stars, mash-up

Compound words: nobody, somebody, another, awesome, something, outside

Grammar and punctuation

Irregular past tense verbs: was, thought, said, took, went, sat, made, read, were, knew, ran, get, felt, kept, sang, stood, held

Adverbs with 'ly' endings: loudly, quickly, wobbly, quietly, happily

Apostrophes for contraction: doesn't, wouldn't, didn't, you're, couldn't, you've, I'm, I'll, it's, don't, he's, you're, I'd, I've, can't, wasn't, we've, what's, you'd, doesn't

Apostrophes for possession: Caplan's, Tom's, Judge's, People's

Questions to interrogate the text

Chapter 1
- Why is Tom having the worst day of his life?
- Why did Jacky ignore Tom?
- What did Tom do to get Jacky's attention?

Chapter 2
- Why doesn't Jacky want to join Tom's band?
- How did Tom change Jacky's mind?
- Why was Jacky fed up after the first practice?

Chapter 3
- Why didn't Jacky's first plan work?
- What was Jacky's second plan?
- What went wrong with Jacky's second plan?

Chapter 4
- What do you think a People's Choice Award is? Why might Tom and Jacky be pleased to win it?
- Why do you think Jacky did not win the main prize?
- Was Jacky pleased to win the People's Choice Award? Why do you think that?

Role-play/drama suggestions

- Discuss Jacky's initial reluctance to join Tom's band. Hold a conscience alley session. One pupil plays Jacky, while the other pupils stand in two lines facing each other. Tell one line to persuade Jacky to concentrate on her own classical performance. Tell the other line to persuade Jacky to help out her friend. At the end, ask Jacky to give her decision and support it with reasons.

- Hot-seat two pupils in the roles of Tom and Jacky. Ask the other pupils to interview them following their success in the competitions.

Copymasters

PCM 1
This copymaster focuses on spelling. Ask the pupils to group the vocabulary given according to the number of syllables.

PCM 2
This copymaster focuses on recall and sequence of events. The correct order is 5, 2, 3, 1, 6, 4.
Talk to the pupils about how the characters feel at each of the events. Ask them to order the events according to the feelings involved.

Counting syllables

Name: _____ Date: _____

Write these words in the boxes to show how many syllables they have. Watch out for words with unstressed syllables, e.g. *diffrent* (diff-e-rent), *evrything* (ev-e-ry-thing).

different	everything	musician	worst	notice	really
competition	thought	bass	piece	violin	listening
other	answer	principal	audience	laughed	February

One syllable

Two syllables

Three syllables

Four syllables

What happened when?

Name: _____   Date: _____

Cut out the statements.
Put them in the right order.

---

1. Jacky rejoins Chasing Trouble.

2. Tom persuades Jacky to replace Taz.

3. Jacky leaves Chasing Trouble.

4. Jacky wins the People's Choice Award.

5. Taz, the double bass player, leaves Chasing Trouble.

6. Chasing Trouble win The People's Choice Award.

How does Tom or Jacky feel at each event?
Put the strips in order to show how Tom or Jacky
feel, starting from 'very bad' through to 'the best'.

| very bad | bad | good | very good | the best |

BAD

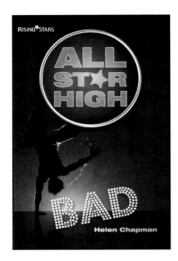

Story summary

Zeke and Becca go busking to raise money so they can go on a school camping trip. Unfortunately, a boy from Zeke's old street gang, Shark, threatens them so Zeke cuts short his busking session. Becca continues but Shark comes back and steals her money. Zeke helps her get away from the gang, but now they only have enough money for one of them to go camping. Later, their friends, the Gang-Stars, join them busking and raise enough money so both Zeke and Becca can go on the trip.

Vocabulary and spelling

Tricky words: reason, either, could, breath, believe, least, nervous, worse, sign, quiet, enough, sweaty, guess

Compound words: backpack, someone, anyone, without, whatever, streetlight, everyone, midday, railway, teenager, afternoon, overhead, something, inside, potatoman, sometimes, courtyard, lunchtime

Hyphenated words: Gang-Stars, under-12s

ea **phoneme** (long *ee* sound): reason, means, least, real, leader, beat, please, jeans, leave, steals, reached, easy, eats

Different pronunciations of the *ea* grapheme: breath, ready, overhead, heavily, sweaty, yeah, great, earn, heard, year, heart, areas, realised

Grammar and punctuation

Irregular past tense verbs: was, saw, got, knew, met, thought, said, kept, felt, took, began, drew, sat, bent, kept, did, had, spat, gave, stood, bit, fell, heard, shook

Adverbs: really, hardly, tightly, heavily, safely, badly, quickly, quietly

Apostrophes for contraction: didn't, couldn't, I'm, it's, don't, doesn't, can't, wasn't, we'll, that's, you'll, we're, you're, let's, he's, I'll, where's, shouldn't, we've, they'll

Apostrophes for possession: Zeke's, Becca's, Shark's

Ellipsis indicating a pause: 'It's just that ...', 'I think we've got about ...'

Italics for emphasis: 'You don't put money *in*. You take it *out*.'

Questions to interrogate the text

Chapter 1
- What feelings did Zeke and Becca have in common that day?
- Why do you think Zeke had kept his grant a secret from the others?
- How did they plan to make some money to pay for the camping trip?

Chapter 2
- Why do you think Zeke was nervous?
- Why did Zeke decide it was time to stop busking?
- What made Zeke change his mind about leaving Becca?

Chapter 3
- When Becca saw Shark had returned, what did she think might happen?
- How did Becca behave towards Shark and his gang?
- What did Zeke do to help Becca escape?

Chapter 4
- Why didn't Becca and Zeke have fun busking in the courtyard?
- How do you think Becca and Zeke felt when Natalie told them what the busking was for?
- What do you think Becca and Zeke learnt from their busking experiences?

Role-play/drama suggestions

- Hot-seat a pupil as Zeke. Invite the other pupils to ask Zeke questions about what happened when he and Becca went busking in Camden. Encourage them to delve into Zeke's different emotions on the day.
- Ask the pupils to work in pairs, one taking the role of Shark and the other taking the role of Natalie's mum. Invite them to role-play what happens when Natalie's mum sees Shark bullying Becca.

Copymasters

PCM 1
This copymaster focuses on apostrophes for contraction. Ask the pupils to rewrite the verb phrases using an apostrophe for contraction, then write the shortened verb phrases in full.

PCM 2
This copymaster involves writing a news report about Natalie's mum's attempt to confront Shark when he stole Becca's money. Discuss the event with the pupils and draw up a list showing their sequence. Go through the typical features of a news report, e.g. a headline, sensational vocabulary, named participants (witnesses). Do they think this is a good or a bad news story? Brainstorm possible catchy headlines, such as 'Have-a-go mum confronts thief'.

Apostrophes

Name: _____ Date: _____

Rewrite these verb phrases using an apostrophe. The first one is done for you.

I cannot	*I can't*		
We are	_____	They will	_____
He would	_____	We will	_____
I do not	_____	We have	_____
You are	_____	He is	_____

Rewrite these shortened verb phrases in full. The first one is done for you.

That's	*That is*		
Let's	_____	We'll	_____
You've	_____	I don't	_____
I can't	_____	We're	_____
He's	_____	I've	_____

News report

Name: _____ Date: _____

Write a news report about Natalie's mum and Shark. Include details to make it exciting for readers.

Headline (short, eye-catching, tells readers what the story is about)

Opening sentence (introduces the story)

What happened? Where and when? Who was involved?

Closing sentence (sum up the story and comment on it)

TROUBLE

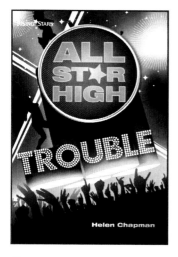

Story summary

Callum and Natalie are both acting in a musical called *Pirates*. Natalie's part is small and she wants to make it special so she brings a parrot to the last rehearsal. At first everyone thinks the parrot is great, until it begins to misbehave and wrecks the costumes. When the performance begins, the audience aren't very impressed, but when the parrot comes on stage they begin to enjoy the show. The parrot is a great success and so is the musical.

Vocabulary and spelling

Tricky words: wrong, voice, pirate, weird, special, thought, sure, audience, people, rehearsal, rehearse, noise, magician, character, sparkle, feathers, fruit, scene, ceiling

Compound words: something, everyone, earrings, sometimes, nobody, anything, cardboard, cannonballs

Hyphenated words: Gang-Stars, Yo-ho-ho, Ta-da, dive-bombed, dressing-room, make-up, dressing-up, long-lost

Exclamations: Avast! Ahoy there! Yo-ho-ho me hearties! Arr, you scurvy dog! Shiver me timbers! Ssh! Be quiet! Ta-da! Wow! Oh no! Pop! Look!

Grammar and punctuation

Irregular past tense verbs: said, had, were, wore, was, thought, made, took, went, began, saw, knew, felt, sang, left, put, flew, heard, did, came, gave

Adverbs: really, hardly, properly, suddenly, badly, politely, only, quickly, wildly, loudly, well

Apostrophes for contraction: what's, don't, I'm, you're, that's, it's, you'll, let's, we'll, can't, I've, wasn't, didn't, I'll, couldn't, he's, she's, I'd, you've, haven't, wouldn't

Apostrophes for possession: Nat's, Gran's, Natalie's, someone's, Fred's, scout's

Questions to interrogate the text

Chapter 1
- Why did Callum think he was the only one asked to be in the contest to play the lead role in the musical *Pirates*?
- What did Callum decide to do to get the lead role and why?
- Why did Natalie learn her lines quickly?

Chapter 2
- How did Natalie bring some sparkle to the musical?
- What happened to Callum when Fred, the parrot, came on stage?
- Why did Callum feel annoyed about Fred?

Chapter 3
- Why did Natalie have to put Fred back in his cage?
- What was the effect of leaving Fred in the dressing-room?
- Why did Natalie say the show was in trouble before it even started?

Chapter 4
- Why did Natalie make up her own lines?
- Why did the audience enjoy the balloons popping?
- How did Natalie and Callum feel about their parts in the musical?

Role-play/drama suggestions

- Encourage the pupils to work in small groups and create a short scene as pirates. Ask them to use 'pirate talk' from the story and to invent some of their own.

- Hot-seat a pupil as Oscar Lee. Invite the other pupils to ask Oscar about his impressions of the musical, including Callum's and Natalie's performances. Ask them to pose questions about Oscar's plans for the parrot's future.

Copymasters

PCM 1
This copymaster focuses on irregular past tense verbs. Pupils change a present tense verb phrase into the past tense.

PCM 2
This copymaster focuses on persuasive writing. Pupils write a letter to Oscar Lee to persuade him that they would be a good parrot-handler and co-star to act in a film with Fred the parrot.

Past tense

Name: _____ Date: _____

Rewrite these present tense verb phrases as past tense verbs. The first one has been done for you.

Present tense	Past tense
I am	*I was*
He does	
You think	
They take	
We see	
She sings	
He hears	
We come	
I give	
We feel	
You know	

A letter to Oscar

Name: _____ Date: _____

Write a letter to Oscar Lee telling him why you should work in a film with Fred the parrot. Give him three good reasons why he should choose you.

Fred the parrot seeks co-star.

Could you star alongside the sensational Fred the parrot?

Dear Oscar,

I feel I am the perfect person to co-star with Fred for the following reasons:

1.

2.

3.

I am sure you would ...

Yours sincerely,

THRILLER

Story summary

It's Halloween and Becca is decorating the school hall for the Zombie Bash. She also decorates an old house next door for the Gang-Stars' own Halloween party. Tom goes to help her and they find a secret passage. While exploring it, four zombies appear. Becca and Tom manage to lock them in the secret passage and escape from the house. On returning to the Zombie Bash, they are about to warn everyone when they see the zombies. They were, in fact, the band that was hired for the school party!

Vocabulary and spelling

Tricky words: thought, bought, voice, disappointed, mouldy, dangerous

Compound words: headstones, graveyard, everything, herself, overgrown, inside, upstairs, downstairs, whatever, nothing, something, anything, nobody, doorway, microphone, everybody

Hyphenated words: Gang-Stars, under-12s, cut-outs, no-one, make-up

Silent letters: design, sign, wrong, knot, stomach, guitars, guessed, heard

igh **phoneme:** high, lighting, might, sighed, light, fright, right, tighter

Grammar and punctuation

Irregular past tense verbs: was, chose, put, said, stood, knew, met, sent, bought, thought, read, took, felt, got, went, lit, slid, shone, ran, became, came, grew, crept, spent, led, found, were, heard

Passive verbs: was held, was chosen, was overgrown, had been decorated, was broken, were covered

Apostrophes for contraction: didn't, couldn't, I'm, it's, don't, doesn't, can't, wasn't, we'll, that's, you'll, we're, you're, let's, he's, I'll, where's, shouldn't, we've, they'll

Speech verbs: said, asked, replied, shouted, cried, stammered, whispered, gasped

Questions to interrogate the text

Chapter 1
- Why did Becca want to borrow some Halloween decorations?
- Where did Becca plan to hold her party?
- Why didn't Tom think he had time to help Becca?

Chapter 2
- Why did Tom think Becca was upstairs?
- Why were Tom and Becca interested in the secret door?
- What did Tom feel about the secret passage?

Chapter 3
- What did Tom and Becca find at the end of the secret passage?
- Why did Tom and Becca think the four figures were zombies?
- How did Tom and Becca escape from the zombies?

Chapter 4
- What did Tom intend to do when he grabbed the microphone?
- When did Tom and Becca realise the zombies were really the band?
- What do you think the flickering light and black shape is?

Role-play/drama suggestions

- Ask pupils to work with a partner. Invite them to imagine they are in a secret passage or tunnel in total darkness. Ask them to role-play finding their way through the passage. Stress that the only senses they can use are hearing and touch.
- Ask pupils to take turns in the hot-seat as Tom and Becca. They should recount their experiences in Rookwood House. Encourage them to describe each other's roles, i.e. Tom describes what Becca did and how she behaved, then vice versa. Tell them to focus on how they felt about what the other person did, e.g. 'Becca was brave when she ...'

Copymasters

PCM 1
This copymaster focuses on active and passive verbs. Pupils change a passive sentence into an active sentence and vice versa.

PCM 2
This copymaster focuses on comprehension. Pupils mark whether the statements about the story are true or false.

Active or passive?

Name: _____ Date: _____

Change these sentences from passive to active or active to passive.
Tip: think about who did the action when changing passive to active.
The first one has been done for you.

Passive	Active
They were terrified of the zombies.	*The zombies terrified them.*
The house was decorated by Becca.	
	A skeleton frightened Tom.
The zombies were locked in the tunnel by Tom.	
A band had already been hired by the teachers.	
	A grinding noise broke the silence.
The mouldy walls were covered with insects.	

True or false?

Name: _____ Date: _____

Show whether these statements are true (✓) or false (✗).

	True or false
Becca chose graveyard props to decorate the hall.	
Becca didn't want any help to decorate Rookwood House.	
Becca was upstairs when Tom went into the house.	
Tom and Becca thought they were trapped in the passage.	
Becca went into the passage so that the zombies would follow her.	
The zombies were the members of the band.	

SUPERSTAR

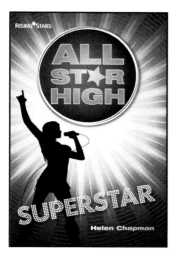

Story summary

Natalie is filmed singing a song by a famous diva, Kira, and doing a vampire dance. It becomes an internet hit and Kira invites her to perform with her on stage. Unfortunately, this clashes with a special school concert Natalie is part of. This upsets the other Gang-Stars, but Natalie still wants to perform with Kira. However, at the last moment, Kira has to cancel her show. When the power fails at the school concert while the other Gang-Stars are performing, Natalie, dressed as a vampire, steps in to save the show.

Vocabulary and spelling

Tricky words: embarrassing, weird, jealous, juice, colour, choirs, orchestra, queue, special, quiet, popular, shrieked, believe, cancelled, audience, guitars

Compound words: nobody, sunlight, everything, nowhere, something, anyone, someone, everywhere, superstar, website, everyone, nowhere, without

Hyphenated words: Gang-Stars, under-12s, blood-red, moon-walked, tongue-tied, make-up

Different ways to pronounce the letters *ie*: tried, tied; friends; believe, shrieked; quiet, amplifier; audience, scariest, spookiest

Grammar and punctuation

Irregular past tense verbs: ran, was, put, met, saw, thought, knew, were, read, got, took, went, set, had, sang, came, found, said, heard, stood, made, began, kept, did

Adverbs: really, quietly, softly, hardly, suddenly, loudly

Apostrophes for contraction: couldn't, didn't, what's, I've, it's, hadn't, wasn't, don't, you're, I'm, wouldn't, mustn't, shouldn't, can't, I'll, that's, isn't, weren't

Apostrophes for possession: Caplan's, Gang-Stars' Nat's, Kira's, Natalie's, producer's, woman's

Italics for emphasis: 'Kira wants *me* to perform with *her*.'

Questions to interrogate the text

Chapter 1
- What did Tom think of his little sister Natalie?
- Why hadn't Tom booked a practice room?
- What did Natalie do to keep up her vampire image?

Chapter 2
- Why was Natalie working hard on her vampire dance?
- What happened to give Tom time to practise drumming?
- How did Natalie react to her dance being filmed?

Chapter 3
- How did Tom feel when Natalie's film was an internet hit? Give two examples.
- How did Natalie feel when Kira phoned her?
- What did Tom and the Gang-Stars think of Natalie's decision to miss the Superstar Spectacular?

Chapter 4
- What happened when the power failed in the Spectacular and what effect did it have?
- How did 'Nat's Bag of Tricks' help to save the Gang-Stars' performance?
- How did Tom's feelings about his sister change from the beginning of the story?

Role-play/drama suggestions

- Hot-seat a pupil as Natalie. Ask the others to interview her about being a vampire. Encourage them to delve into Natalie's motives and feelings. What things did she do? Why did she want to act as a vampire? How did other people react to her and how did she feel about it?

- Ask the pupils to work in small groups. Invite them to imagine that a film of a close friend becomes an internet hit. Give them different emotions – happy, proud, envious, jealous, angry. Ask them to choose one emotion each and role-play a conversation when they meet to discuss their friend's success.

Copymasters

PCM 1
This copymaster focuses on adjectives. Ask the pupils to add suffixes of degree (*–er/–est*) to adjectives from the story. They should write a sentence that uses each adjective.

PCM 2
This copymaster focuses on a sequence of events. Pupils match the events to a timeline for the story. The correct order is 2, 7, 1, 3, 5, 4, 8, 6.

Adding suffixes

Name: _____ Date: _____

Add the suffixes –er and –est to these adjectives. The first one has been done for you.

pale	paler	palest
weird		
spooky		
scary		
crazy		
big		
spiky		

Now write a sentence for each using the three adjectives. One has been done as an example.

Tom's face is pale, Kira's face is paler but Natalie's face is the palest.

_____

_____

_____

_____

_____

Timeline

Name: _____ Date: _____

Match these events to the timeline. Write in the number of the sentence on the timeline. One example has been done for you.

Start of the story   **End of the story**

2							

1. A boy with spiky red hair makes a film of Natalie's dance.

2. Natalie tells Tom about the Superstar Spectacular.

3. Kira invites Natalie to perform with her in a show.

4. The power fails during the Gang-Stars performance.

5. Kira cancels the show.

6. Natalie decides to stop being a vampire.

7. Natalie lets Tom practise his singing and drumming while she practises dancing.

8. Natalie welcomes the audience to the Gang-Stars Fright Fest.

RESCUE

Story summary

A new talent academy has opened near All Star High and Claire is afraid it will become bigger and better than her own school. So when Claire and Callum go to a Saturday morning rehearsal and see people waiting to tour the new academy standing outside their school by mistake, Claire decides to give them a tour of All Star High instead. Mrs Benson, the mother of two reality show winners, has a small dog which gets trapped in a prop for their show *Titanic*. Claire rescues the dog, saving both the pet and All Star High.

Vocabulary and spelling

Tricky words: worried, wrong, theatre, nudged, people, whimper, pressure, calm, concentrate, aisle

Compound words: outside, something, everything, someone, online, updates, backstage, website, floorboard

Nouns naming types of people with 'or' and 'er' endings: actor, dancer, singers, visitors, reporters

Grammar and punctuation

Speech verbs: grumbled, wondered, asked, said, went on, whispered, mumbled, explained, hissed, called, cried, moaned, shouted, thought, reminded

Adverbs: really, only, politely, sweetly, quickly, suddenly, easily, carefully

Literal and figurative use of verbs: The ship was rocking!, 'That rocked!' said Zane.

Questions to interrogate the text

Chapter 1
- Why was Claire worried by the Talent Academy?
- Why did Claire decide to give the visitors a tour of her school?
- Why do you think Callum was against taking the visitors around the school?

Chapter 2
- What do you think Zane and Zara were thinking and feeling when Claire refused to make the model ship rock?

- Why did Zane and Zara want to be filmed on the rocking ship?
- Why did they start playing/rocking the ship as soon as the fans and reporters arrived in the theatre?

Chapter 3
- Why do you think Callum decided not to tell off Zane and Zara, or switch off the ship?
- Why didn't the twins want to be filmed with their mother?
- How did Claire feel when she went into the ship to rescue Ginger?

Chapter 4
- Why did Callum think Claire was starting to panic?
- Why weren't the reporters interested in Zane and Zara?
- What did Mrs Benson mean by 'training for real life'?

Role-play/drama suggestions

- Hot-seat a pupil as Claire and ask her to recount the tour of the school. Encourage the others to imagine they are the reporters. Ask them to question Claire about her motives and feelings, particularly those relating to the school and her experience while rescuing Ginger.
- Split the class into small groups. Invite a volunteer from each group to act as a guide. Tell them to give the rest of the group a guided tour around the classroom or part of the school. Encourage the guide to make positive comments so that the others see the classroom or school as a place they would like to attend.

Copymasters

PCM 1
This copymaster focuses on spelling. Pupils add –er or –or to verbs to make the name of someone who performs an action or activity.

PCM 2
This copymaster focuses on writing a poster to advertise an open day for All Star High School.

Making nouns

Name: _____ Date: _____

A walker is a person who walks. Add the correct ending *–er* or *–or* to these verbs to make the name of a person who does the activity.

Passive	–er or –or
write	
sing	
dance	
visit	
teach	
report	
play	
read	
edit	
act	

Come to All Star High!

Name: _____ Date: _____

All Star High is having an open day. Design a poster to advertise the event. Remember to keep the information brief. Attract people's attention and make them want to visit the school.

What is happening?

When and where?

What will visitors see or experience?

Why should people come?

FIGHT

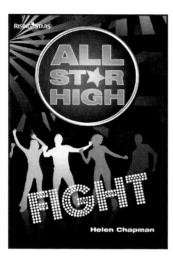

Story summary

Aaron is really keen on martial arts, but no-one else at school is. He gets a big surprise when the new dance teacher encourages him to mix his martial arts steps with dance steps. He gets an even bigger surprise when he is given the role of Romeo in the ballet *Romeo and Juliet*. Claire is really keen on being a ballerina, but despite being given the role of Juliet, she isn't happy that it is a modern ballet. She and Aaron fall out about the way they are supposed to dance until they finally join forces to work out new steps.

Vocabulary and spelling

Tricky words: martial, would, thought, ridiculous, famous, seriously, mirrors, sighed, choice, favourite, rehearsal, beautiful, circus, relief

Compound words: nobody, drawstring, handrail, anything, everything, kickboxing, workshops

Hyphenated words: warm-up, T-shirt, Gang-Stars, under-12s, mid-air, real-life

Different ways to pronounce the letters *ie*: replied, tried; Juliet, aliens, audience; believe, hurried, families, married, worried, relief, Natalie

Grammar and punctuation

Irregular past tense verbs: had, was, got, wore, thought, sent, knew, did, took, were, felt, stood, put, came, burst, spoke, went, let, caught, ran

Vivid action verbs: yelled, burst out, shuffled, kicked, hissed, leapt, hanging, freeze, spinning, swinging, fall, twirled, sweep, grabbed, squirted, chased, danced, leaped, laughed

Apostrophes for contraction: wasn't, he'd, we're, I'm, shouldn't, didn't, won't, that's, they're, don't, we've, you'll, couldn't, I'll, aren't, it's, wouldn't, can't, you're, I've, he's, there's, we'd

Apostrophes for possession: Aaron's, High's, Claire's, other's, clown's

Questions to interrogate the text

Chapter 1
- In what ways did the new dance teacher, Mr Jay, surprise the students?
- How did Claire feel about getting the role of Juliet?
- How did Claire feel about Aaron getting the role of Romeo and why?

Chapter 2
- In what ways did Claire and Aaron respond to the idea of playing aliens?
- How did Claire react to being told to learn Aaron's dance moves?
- Why did Claire decide to stop fighting with Aaron?

Chapter 3
- What was the purpose of going to see the Circus Acrobats?
- Why do you think Claire went red?
- How did Claire and Aaron feel when Mr Jay thought their idea was amazing?

Chapter 4
- What did the other Gang-Stars think of Claire and Aaron's routine?
- Why do you think Aaron said he would 'just slime her'?
- What did Natalie mean when she said 'we've got a real-life Romeo and Juliet here'?

Role-play/drama suggestions

- In small groups, ask the pupils to work out a short dance while moving like aliens. Invite the groups to perform their alien dances for each other.
- Hot-seat a pupil in the role of Claire. Ask the others to imagine they are newspaper reporters interviewing Claire after her performance, for a theatre review in a newspaper.

Copymasters

PCM 1

This copymaster focuses on compound words. Ask the pupils to cut out the word cards and combine them to make compound words. They should write sentences for three compound words.

PCM 2

This copymaster focuses on writing a newspaper review of All Star High's production of *Romeo and Juliet*. Pupils use a writing frame to write the review.

Compound words

Name: _____ *Date:* _____

Cut out the word cards. Put two cards together to make a compound word. How many compound words can you make? Write sentences for three of the compound words.

any	thing
some	every
no	where
one	body

1. _____

2. _____

3. _____

A night at the theatre

Name: _____ Date: _____

Imagine you are a theatre critic! Write a review of All Star High's production of *Romeo and Juliet*.

Introduce the review.	*All Star High School staged a production of Romeo and Juliet last night in the school's theatre.*
How was the production different from a traditional ballet?	
Who danced the leading roles?	
How did the audience react?	
Who produced (organised) the show?	
Make a personal comment about the show. How much did you enjoy it and why?	

SHOUT!

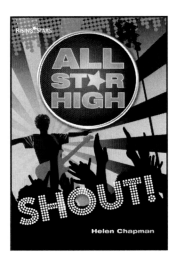

Story summary

Callum Murphy and Aaron Farmer are cousins and friends at All Star High. Callum is the best singer and actor in the school. Aaron can act and sing but is really better at dancing. They both try out in the auditions for the musical *Oliver*. A famous singer and actor comes to the auditions to find a star for a West End show. But Callum's voice begins to break and he cannot shout, so Aaron helps him out. Neither one gets the West End part but they both work so well together that they get parts in a charity show instead.

Vocabulary and spelling

Tricky words: worst, friends, jealous, rehearsal, sure, martial, audition, special

Silent letters *wh, ch*: wreck, whispered, wrong, character

Compound words: something, everything, sometimes, anyway, everyone, anyone

Hyphenated words: Gang-Stars, under-12s, no-one, pick-pocket

Different pronunciations of *ough* letters: thought, though, cough, enough, through

Grammar and punctuation

Irregular past tense verbs: thought, met, were, had, was, said, felt, tried, came, could, went, got, stood, worried, knew, made, gave, read, hopped, saw, ran, put, threw, understood, heard, found, meant, forgot, lost, did

Adverbs: really, usually, quietly, quickly, properly, perfectly, cheekily

Apostrophes for contraction: I've, that's, they're, I'm, wasn't, doesn't, what's, I'll, wouldn't, couldn't, it's, don't, you're, you'd, didn't, hadn't, he's, what's, let's, can't, it'll, mustn't, won't, you'll, he'd, I'd

Apostrophes for possession: Aaron's, Callum's, Lukas's

Questions to interrogate the text

Chapter 1
- Why did Callum think Oliver was a good musical for the school to put on?
- What did Callum think was happening to his voice?
- What made Callum worry about the audition?

Chapter 2
- What made Aaron think he had a chance in the audition for the role of Oliver Twist?
- How did Aaron feel about his audition?
- What three ways did Aaron try to help Callum?

Chapter 3
- What did Callum mean when he told Aaron to 'be his voice'?
- How did the help Aaron gave to Callum affect his own chances in the first rehearsal?
- When Aaron was sent off the stage, what did he decide to do and why?

Chapter 4
- Why did Callum stop in the middle of his performance?
- Why do you think Lukas told Callum and Aaron that they weren't ready for a West End show yet?
- Why do you think Lukas invited the two boys to take part in a charity show with him?

Role-play/drama suggestions

- Discuss Callum's attitude to his talent. Hold a conscience alley session. One pupil plays Callum while the other pupils stand in two lines facing each other. Ask one line to encourage Callum and give reasons why his attitude is fine. The other line should try to show Callum his attitude is arrogant.

- Discuss why Callum was so confident about his acting and singing abilities. Invite the pupils to work with a partner and discuss the abilities they feel proud of. If they are slow to think of any, you could suggest things such as sports, dancing, cycling, singing, playing games, being a good friend, looking after a brother or sister, etc. Ask each pupil to give a short description of one of their partner's abilities and why they are good at it.

Copymasters

PCM 1
This copymaster focuses on spelling when adding a suffix to a verb. Ask the pupils to add the suffixes *–ing* and *–ed* to the verbs.

PCM 2
This copymaster focuses on adjectives to describe character. Discuss the personalities of Callum and Aaron. Invite the pupils to suggest words that describe each of them. Ask them to say whether Callum changed during the story and if so how. Ask the pupils to draw a line to link the adjectives to Callum or Aaron. Explain that some adjectives may apply to both characters.

Adding suffixes

Name: _____ Date: _____

Add the suffixes to the verbs.

	-ing	-ed
try	trying	tried
worry		
make		
hope		
nod		
grin		
excite		
surprise		

Adjectives

Name: _____ Date: _____

Draw a line to link the adjectives to the character.

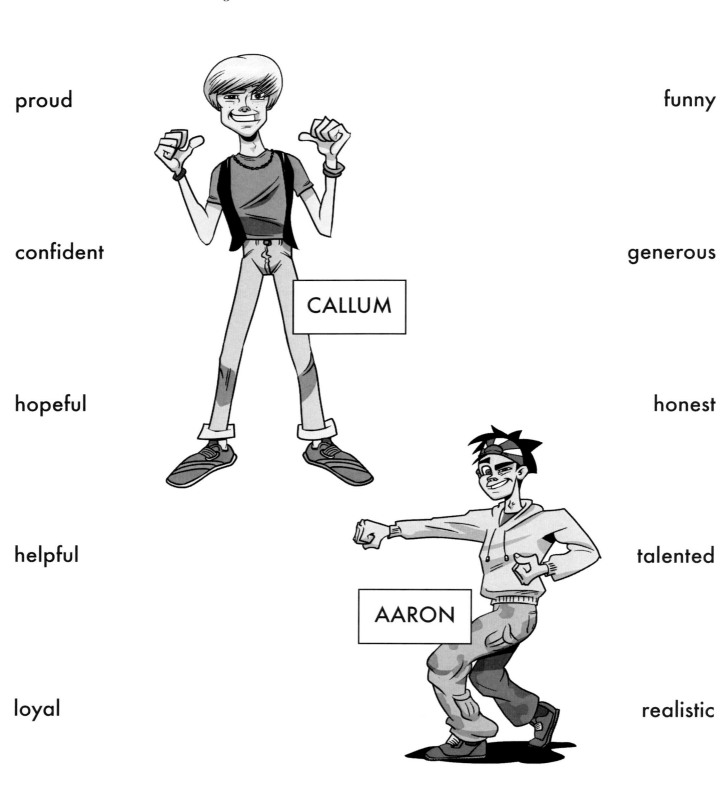

proud

confident

hopeful

helpful

loyal

funny

generous

honest

talented

realistic

CALLUM

AARON

CRIMINAL

Story summary

All the Gang-Stars have had things stolen from their lockers, except Zeke. Jacky is worried that Zeke might be the thief, and when Principal Blake has a locker inspection, the stolen property is found in Zeke's locker. Zeke and Jacky try to find out who the thief is. When Principal Blake's laptop is stolen, they can prove it wasn't Zeke.

Vocabulary and spelling

Silent letters: sign, listening, wrong, friends, guilty

ie **as** *ee* **phenome:** thief, ceiling, believe

Words ending in *-tion***:** inspection, explanation

Compound words: something, everyone, someone, drumstick, anything, everything, shoplifting, whoever, anyone, headphones, videotape, nobody

Hyphenated words: Gang-Stars, under-12s, back-up, no-one, twenty-four

Grammar and punctuation

Irregular past tense verbs: was, said, were, met, rang, got, had, thought, knew, took, left, heard, felt, went, began, held

Verbs ending 'y' rule for adding suffix *–ed***:** tried, worried, cried, replied

Fragments/incomplete sentences: 'No, not everyone.' 'Just the members of the Gang-Stars.' 'Not just his place at All Star High, but all his friends too.'

Questions to interrogate the text

Chapter 1
- Why was Jacky in a panic?
- What made Jacky suspicious of Zeke?
- Why did Jacky worry that Zeke was the thief?

Chapter 2
- Who do you think was listening to Jacky and Zeke?
- Why do you think someone was waiting for Principal Blake to open Zeke's locker?
- How did the other Gang-Stars feel when Zeke went to Principal Blake's office?

Chapter 3
- Why was Jacky sure that Zeke couldn't be the thief?
- Why were they unable to recognise the thief?
- Why didn't Principal Blake just accept Zeke and Jacky's ideas about the thief?

Chapter 4
- Why did Mr Newman threaten to give the lead dancer role to someone else?
- How were Zeke and Jacky able to prove they were innocent?
- Why do you think the thief targeted Zeke?

Role-play/drama suggestions

- Hot-seat a pupil as Simon, the thief. Invite the other pupils to ask Simon questions about why he stole from the Gang-Stars. You may want them to work in small groups first to think of their questions. Encourage them to delve into Simon's motives for stealing and setting up Zeke as the culprit. Ask them to find out how Simon feels now that he has been caught.

- Ask groups to role-play being the Gang-Stars as they open up their lockers and discover they have been robbed. Tell them to freeze-frame the moment of discovery. Ask them each to say what they are thinking and feeling.

Copymasters

PCM 1

This copymaster focuses on adding suffixes to verbs ending in 'y'. Pupils add the *–ed* and *–ing* suffixes to ten verbs to change them into continuous present and past tense forms. They should circle the verbs that do not conform to the rule – *drop 'y' and add –ied for past tense verbs.*

PCM 2

This copymaster focuses on writing a persuasive letter from Simon to the principal. Pupils should write from Simon's point of view to try and explain why he should not be expelled from school.

Present and past tense

Rewrite these verbs ending in 'y' as continuous present tense and past tense verbs. The first one has been done for you. Circle the past tense verbs that do not end in -ied.

I try	I am trying	I tried
I reply		
I spy		
I fly		
I buy		
I dry		
I study		
I hurry		
I marry		
I annoy		
I pray		

Simon's letter

Name: _____ *Date:* _____

Imagine you are Simon. Write a letter to Principal Blake to persuade him to let you stay at All Star High School.

1. Describe how sorry you are.
2. Explain why you want to stay at the school.
3. Describe what you will do in the future.
4. Summarise how you feel about what you did.

Dear Principal Blake,

I am writing to ask you not to expel me.

1. _____

   _____

2. _____

   _____

3. _____

   _____

4. _____

   _____

Yours sincerely,

Simon

FAME

Story summary

Zeke and Aaron both think there is an audition happening for a new dance show on TV. Throughout the day, they try to find time to rehearse but things keep going wrong. Eventually they find out they were set up by the other Gang-Stars for a TV show called *Tricked You!*. They will get on TV after all, just not in the way they wanted!

Vocabulary and spelling

Tricky words: television, fountain, believe, audition, techno, notice, trouble, disappeared, basins, mirrors, colour, suggested, sweat, favourite

Compound words: lunchtime, classrooms, courtyard, someone, something, hairdresser, fingernails, outside

Hyphenated words: kick-boxing, make-up, no-one, mix-up, Gang-Stars, under-12s

Different pronunciations of the letters *ea*:

***ee* phoneme:** each, teacher, please, leave, easy, clean, neat, seats, cream, freak, scream, streaks, mean

short e phoneme: read, instead, wear, yeah, heads, already, heavy, spread, sweat, ready, breath

***ur* phoneme:** rehearsal, heard

***ai* phoneme:** great, break

Other pronunciations: really, area, idea

Grammar and punctuation

Speech verbs: said, asked, replied, started, grumbled, cried out, suggested, called out, shouted, wailed

Rhetorical questions: Who cares? But why? But who? What if the chairs disappeared again? What if our mates see us?

Exclamations: Hey, look! Loser! Oh no! Smile! Ewwww!

Questions to interrogate the text

Chapter 1
- What was unusual about the notice on the gym door?
- What happened after Zeke and Aaron set out the chairs in the courtyard?
- Why do Zeke and Aaron think someone wants them

to get into trouble?

Chapter 2
- Why did Miss Walker tell Zeke and Aaron to go to the hair and make-up classroom?
- Why did Zeke and Aaron go to the bike sheds?
- What do you think might be significant about the van?

Chapter 3
- How do Zeke and Aaron feel about having their hair and nails done?
- How did Zeke and Aaron react to having pink hair?
- What excuse did Kate give for using hair dye? Do you think it was a genuine mistake? Why?

Chapter 4
- Why did Zeke and Aaron think something was wrong when they got to the dance studio?
- How do you think they felt as soon as they knew they had been tricked?
- Do you think they forgave the other Gang-Stars? What makes you think that?

Role-play/drama suggestions

- Invite the pupils to work in groups of four to re-enact the scene in the hair and make-up classroom. Remind them that Kate and Meg know about the trick but Aaron and Zeke do not know yet.
- Ask the pupils to work in small groups. They should collaborate on a conversation about Miss Walker and the other Gang-Stars planning to trick Aaron and Zeke. Allow them sufficient time to make notes before inviting them to share the role-play conversation.

Copymasters

PCM 1
This copymaster focuses on punctuation. Pupils add either a question mark or an exclamation mark to sentences and phrases from the story.

PCM 2
This copymaster focuses on writing a review of All Star High's production of Romeo and Juliet. Pupils use a writing frame to write a newspaper review.

? or !

Name: _____ Date: _____

Read the phrases and sentences. Add a question mark ? or an exclamation mark !.
Check the story to help you.

1. 'This audition is our big chance to be famous ☐ '

2. 'What if our mates see us ☐ '

3. 'Loser ☐ '

4. 'Oh no ☐ ' they cried out.

5. 'What's going on ☐ ' asked Zeke.

6. No way ☐ Tricked You ☐ is my favourite TV show ☐

7. 'You mean this is all a joke ☐ There is no dance show ☐ ' asked Zeke.

8. 'Ewwww ☐ ' wailed Jacky and Natalie.

Story mountain

Name: _____ *Date:* _____

Most story plots have four main parts: a beginning, build-up, climax and ending.
Look carefully at *Fame*. Can you find these four parts of the story?
Write a few words about the story on the story mountain.

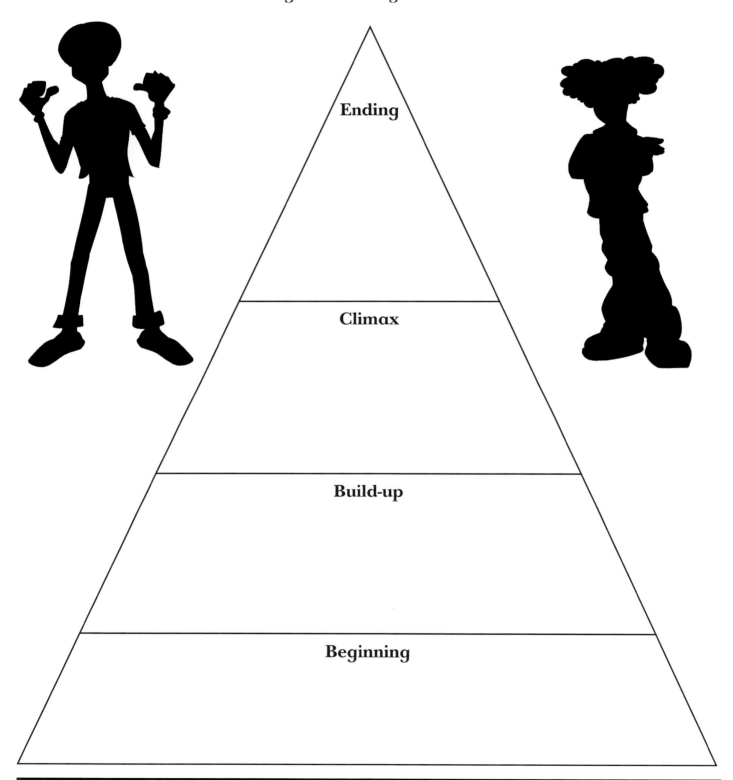

Ending

Climax

Build-up

Beginning

Reading record

Name: _____ *Date:* _____

Complete your own All Star High reading record using this chart.
Mark your favourite book with a star.

Book title	Date read	Marks out of 10	Comments
HELP!			
BAD			
TROUBLE			
THRILLER			
SUPERSTAR			
RESCUE			
FIGHT			
SHOUT!			
CRIMINAL			
FAME			

All Star High: Reading record PCM

Character cards

Cut out these character cards to remind you who is who. Use the blank card to create your own new character or to include yourself!

Aaron	Callum
Jacky	Claire
Tom	Natalie
Zeke	Becca
Mystery kid	_____